The Book of Daddyisms

DeShaun N. Wise Porter
Keith Evan Wise

13TH & JOAN

For permission requests, write to the publisher, addressed "Attention: Permissions Coordinator," 205 N. Michigan Avenue, Suite #810, Chicago, IL 60601. 13th & Joan books may be purchased for educational, business or sales promotional use. For information, please email the Sales Department at sales@13thandjoan.com.

Printed in the U. S. A.

First Printing, June 2023.

Library of Congress Cataloging-in-Publication Data has been applied for.

ISBN: 978-1-953156-78-5

Dedication

From DeShaun

To my Dad, Keith Evan Wise. There is nothing more precious in a young girl's life than her dad. He is her protector, her hero, and her very first love. The bond, unbreakable. The memories, timeless. The love, immeasurable. Dad, thank you for loving me unconditionally and teaching me to soar like an eagle. For all the times you thought I wasn't listening, this is for you.

To the girls who may never know the love of a Father or father-figure, I share these words of wisdom with you. May they embrace you, encourage you, and inspire you.

To the guys who are Fathers or aspire to be a great Father, never stop instilling the very best in your children. Even when you think they are not listening, they are. Even when you think they are not watching, they are. May your actions speak louder than your words, but may your words be a mirror to your actions.

From Keith

This book is dedicated to my incredible daughter who listened, and to my grandsons Princeton and Braylon, whose walk in life will be Godly inspired. It is my prayer that each of you will find your Superpowers to help make the World a Better Place.

Foreword

When I had the pleasure of reading *A Book of Daddyisms* from my Goddaughter to her Dad, deep inside my being I could feel an overwhelming sense of gratitude and profoundness. The words from a daughter back to her father. Simply saying that you may not have known it while you were given out those words of wisdom, but that you've taken them deep within me every time you ushered those simple words that either uplifted me, consoled me, or gave me courage no matter what I was going through. Often those words can be a turning point in one's life, and often those words of wisdom have been handed down to people from their parents and grandparents and just those wiser, older people in their lives. The elders were meant to dispense wisdom and most importantly, common sense. Or simply offer words of advice to someone struggling through an adverse situation.

When you look at where idioms and parables began, you will find that they have been around since people have been around. We know that Jesus spoke in parables in many of his sermons. The "early bird catches the worm" first showed up in the 1600s. It was said by William Camden and it simply means that you have a better chance at success if you get a head start. Get there before everyone else if you want the best chance at succeeding. These simple yet profound words were probably handed down to him through a father or grandparent. These words, like those in *A Book of Daddyisms*, had to be powerful and pretty simple so that people, or rather younger people, would remember them. The more they heard them and listened to them the more they took them to heart. And even more importantly, they passed them on to their children. They in turn became a part of our lives and our constitution, and often added deeper meaning to our lives. They became the foundation that would get us through some of our most difficult times. And at other times they would just come to us at odd moments and bring a smile to our face. If you're of a certain age you grew up with these parables. If you're a lot younger, take to heart the fact that DeShaun listened to these throughout the years and remembered them and is now sharing her gift with us. They have given her life such a powerful foundation. At my very core it's my mother telling me to be kind to everyone I meet. She'd say, "even a dog can wag its tail when it passes you on the street." Those words I've carried with me all through my life and they have shaped my life more than I can tell you. Remember that for the most part these parables were said before people were reading and writing, so they had to be told so that people would remember them, and not only remember, but take them in and at some point give to others so that their life might be changed. DeShaun has written them down and is now sharing them so that each of us may have a chance to take them in, and they just might feed our inner spirit, which may in turn give our life more meaning. Remember, at first glance, it might not make sense, it's upon further reflection that the meaning will come to you. I can't thank you enough for embarking on this journey.

Howard "H" White
Founder of Believe to Achieve Foundation,
Senior Vice President,
Brand Jordan at NIKE,
Author of Believe to Achieve

Preface

This book is inspired by my father who is known for his random words of wisdom. These pages are a collection of early morning wake-up calls with words of wisdom, random text messages, emails, lunch dates, Sunday dinners, and mid-day conversations compiled over the course of several years. If they were sent via text or email, they are preserved here in their original state so embrace the ALL CAPS – he was not yelling, but that was a common approach he used when trying to get my attention. For some messages, I shared the prompt to provide you with greater context to my frame of mind at the time and my father's motivational response. For others, there was no prompt and the magic is that the message was still right on time. No lead up conversation, no off-putting disposition at the dinner table – just a

Daddy randomly speaking from the heart and knowing exactly what "Princess" needed to hear. As you indulge in reading this book, "Princess" will appear many times throughout, as that is my father's name for me. If needed, feel free to adapt the message so that these words can be as motivational to you as they are to me.

My father is a conversationalist at heart with the smile of a gentle giant. He has a knack for asking questions that could disarm a caged soul and is always sharing words of inspiration, hope, and courage to all he meets. As a receiver of his wisdom, I now share it with you. If I had a penny for every time he told me to, "write [it] down" his daddyisms, I'd be one rich woman. Well, here's to being one rich woman!

CHAPTER ONE

A Daily Dose of Wisdom

When you're angry but need to reassess your emotions...

"Every day you have a finite amount of intellectual property and emotional currency, don't waste it on situations that will bring back zero return on your investment."

When you're struggling to accept that things do not always happen on your time...

"Nothing happens before its time, but you can't sit idle, so get up – you still have a part to play!!"

When you need a reminder on safety...

**"You are loved!!!!!!!!
Don't drive and text, it can wait."**

"Hold this in your heart and understand that life is full of distractions designed to knock you off your course. Be Smart, Stay Focused, and Stay Committed. Remember, 'The race is not given to the swift nor the strong, but to those who endure to the end.' Ecclesiastes 9:11

Translation: "Success is built on focus and perseverance!!"

When it rains and it pours....

**"NEVER DOUBT,
NEVER QUESTION,
RELY ON YOUR FAITH TO PULL YOU
THROUGH ROUGH TIMES!!!!"**

15

When your self-confidence is unstable...

"Your life's journey has been shaped by the people that LOVE you. They have instilled in you the Courage, Discipline, Faith, Love, and Humility for you to believe in your skill sets that you have developed on your own.

The end result may not always be a 'win,' but the achievement of not shying away from the challenge will strengthen you, and in the end make you stronger for the task ahead."

Yoda: "Do or not do, there is no try." "BE COMMITTED!!"

When things don't go quite as planned...

"Failure is a predicate to my success. Persistence is my gift."

When you need a reminder
to just keep going...

**"When you were
running as a little girl
and fell, did you get
up? When you fell off
the bike, did you get
back on? Every lesson
in life has a meaning.
You have already
become a champion
in perseverance, just
reflect on your life."**

**"Remember Grandma
saying,
'YOU CAN DO IT!!!!!!'"**

"On the other side of any challenge is success. You have developed a sense of work ethic, determination (funny face), integrity, purpose, and a vision that will carry you through. Stay the course."

Fun Fact: my dad is still learning to use emojis – instead he writes it out as seen above.

"Princess, here is a quote
attributable to an unknown
author but extremely applicable
in various situations."

"Excellence is the result of caring more than
others think is wise
Risking more than others think is safe
Dreaming more than others think is practical,
and expecting more than others think
is possible"

23

"Here is your personal arsenal of power words and phrases that will never let you down and will help you through good and bad times:

'God's Got This'

God made the stars and the heavens, the sunshine and the rain for us. If He has done all of that, He will not let me fail.

Faith:

An intangible aspect that, if grasped, is a powerful tool that allows us an extension and connection to the true Power Source in our life.

Love:

An intangible aspect that is given to us at birth. A baby radiates the essence of love, one hundred percent reliant on others but one hundred percent giving in its simplest aspect (A SMILE).

Smile and Laughter:

It dissipates tension, lightens moods, brings JOY. A powerful human component.

Integrity:

This is the moral fiber that is an essential component which defines character, and this is who you ARE.

Morality:

Discerning right from wrong and good from bad is a parent's responsibility to instill as one of a child's guardrails as they develop in life. It is up to you to incorporate it into your basic fiber and character.

Discipline:
A guardrail that parents must instill for you to reach your goals in life. It happens throughout your childhood and if you grasp it, your success is insured.

Empathy and Generosity:
These critical human emotions MUST always be in the forefront of your decision-making process. Everyone has different strengths and weaknesses. Your awareness of those will make you an outstanding leader because you will ALWAYS ask people to do what they do best, and they will respond.

Work Ethic and Commitment:
If it is worth doing, then it is worth doing well. Always clearly define your goal before you start. There will be headwinds on any endeavor but lock in and 'GET THERE.'

Grandma would always say, '**YOU CAN DO IT**.'

Belief:
Confidence is instilled from toddler to senior citizen. Confidence is both verbal and non-verbal, so always be extremely careful what you say. The impact of a negative word can last a lifetime.

Plan for Success:
Life is a game of chess. Some may use the word strategic. Success is not an accident, it is a combination of everything above plus more. Confidence comes from employing these components repeatedly until they become a part of your DNA.

Motivation is simple. An implanted idea occurs in a dream or elsewhere, and when it is time, you will move forward to realize it in your life. As a wise man once said, 'nothing happens before its time.'"

"I HONOR THE GREATEST GIFT THAT GOD HAS GIVEN US, AND THAT IS UNCONDITIONAL LOVE.

Love is the wonderment of life and the internal treasure that resides in each of us.

God never yells, so why should we at each other?

The truth always reveals itself if we are quiet and listen. It is human nature to do otherwise, but the answer is/was within you.

God loves everyone, but He only chose a close 12. Follow His lead and be selective.

We learn best when we are quiet, there may be a reason why we have two ears and one mouth.

Attribute every good thing that happens as a blessing or miracle. If done, it will increase your capacity to be humble, which is an attribute."

When you need to manage your
temper to increase your impact...

**"A soft word carries infinitely more power
and impact than yelling, which only obscures
the message."**

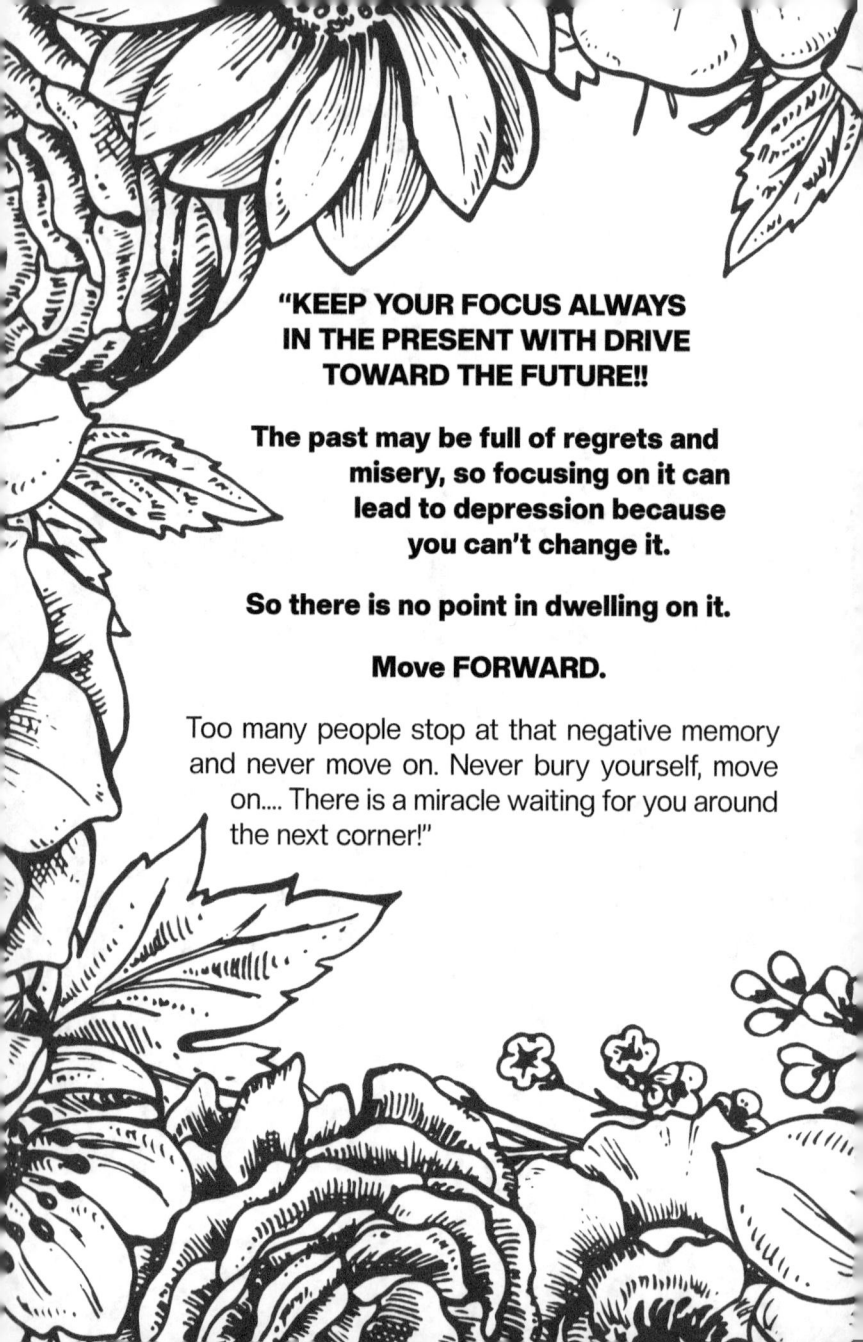

"KEEP YOUR FOCUS ALWAYS IN THE PRESENT WITH DRIVE TOWARD THE FUTURE!!

The past may be full of regrets and misery, so focusing on it can lead to depression because you can't change it.

So there is no point in dwelling on it.

Move FORWARD.

Too many people stop at that negative memory and never move on. Never bury yourself, move on.... There is a miracle waiting for you around the next corner!"

When it's time to make a decision...

"A good decision is 51/49.
- Grandpa"

"Follow the basic principles of God first, family second, and career, friends, and country, third. Prayer will give you the confidence and courage to make the best decision for you."

When you are assessing your options...

"Eagles always see the possibilities before eliminating choices."

"Eagles have visions that arise only after the hard work of getting to the highest place possible. Eagles fail in their hunt for game more often than they succeed. The key is that each attempt makes their wings stronger and their bodies more muscular."

"Choose wisely on which endeavors you select. Partial effort guarantees partial success."

"Don't use normal judgment in
abnormal times, it will throw you off
and you will misread the actions.

Anger and unsettling times are unwelcome
storms in life, BUT they do happen. Anger is
personal and unavoidable in life. How we see
things narrows down to how we see the world
at that moment. Do we see it as events that are
blessings or do we see it as burdens? Never
make decisions when the burden mentality is
dominant. This will only lead to more issues and
extend the period of disturbance. In the short
term, it never pans out. Be your own hero and
stop the chaos as soon as possible.

Long term decisions are best made when
you are in a 'blessings' mindset, so why
not make camp and stay there?"

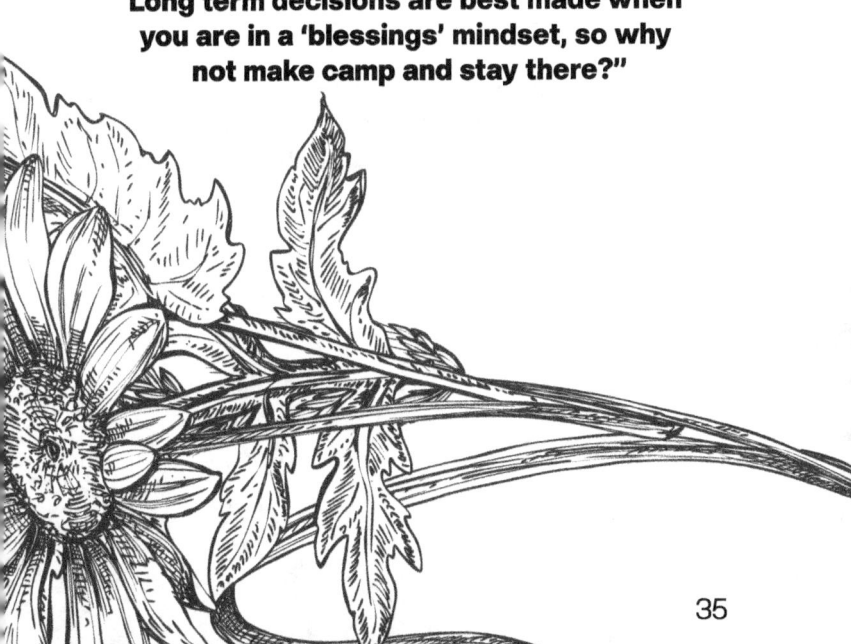

**"Don't doubt yourself and definitely don't doubt God...
Some of God's best work happens when things seem impossible."**

"Princess, when things are tough, as sometimes life brings issues, never forget that you too are a miracle. Think of the amazement that touched you when you saw an incredible sunset. Who provided that?

Think of the view from the balcony in Ocean City as the sun sets? Who provided that?

Think of walking in France, alone, in your young twenties. Who provided you with the confidence to navigate those streets and protected you in a country where you knew no one?

The Lesson: When in doubt know this, if I can't, the family can't, He Can and always has. Rest assured and be comforted with that knowledge."

"Make the impossible possible."

"You have grown up to be an
incredible daughter, an
awesome wife, and
now God has gifted
you as a Mother.

You have made the
IMPOSSIBLE, possible!!!!!!!!"

"Eagles soar. So
don't let pigeons
bring you down."

"Eagles give
people inspiration.
Everyone looks up
when they see an Eagle
soar. You can't solve other
people's problems, but you can
leave them inspired and it is NON-
Verbal. A HUG, A SMILE, A NOD!!!!!"

On having empathy but not feeling
responsible for everyone's problems...

**"Believe in people so that they believe in
themselves. The results of their journey is
theirs and theirs alone. You are not responsible
for their success or their demise."**

On days when you want to quit...

"Just keep going! No progress has ever been made by just standing still."

"Do you remember the last time you quit something? Chances are you really weren't committed in the beginning... BUT IF IT IS IMPORTANT, LIKE DADDY, TAKE OFF YOUR WATCH AND GET IT DONE!!!!"

If you can be anyone...

**"Be a Friday type of person.
Friday people are happy people.
Be happy."**

"People are like days of the week and how you can identify them.

Monday, Tuesday people/personalities are always either down or griping about something. You may have to work with them, but don't bring them into your circle.

Wednesday people/personalities are always non-committal. You can give this type of person a million dollars or take a million dollars away and they would be unmoved. We are human beings and need feedback. You may work with them, but don't include them in your close circle.

Thursday people are moody but extremely necessary because they are either excited about the weekend or depressed because nothing is happening. These people are necessary in your circle because they are the straws that help stir the drink.

Friday people have the right mindset for life. They are usually energetic, thoughtful, and get more things accomplished in a shorter period of time. Additionally, they create a great work environment. That philosophy means they con-centrate on the day and plan for tomorrow. It's a great attitude!!

The key to life is to surround yourself with Friday-minded people."

On being selective about the company you keep...

"Steer clear of anyone who has a problem for every solution. They will only bring you down."

"Princess, I have NEVER seen a pessimist discover anything. If you don't climb the mountain, YOU CAN'T SEE THE VIEW!!!!!!"

On overcoming the fear of flying...

"I didn't know you would take being an eagle seriously. To the girl who was once scared to fly – now the world is her backyard, her feet - never on the floor, and when she's awake, the world is her stage."

"Princess, how you overcame that fear of flying has led you to fly all over the world. Like an eagle, you are inspirational in what you have overcome through the WORK ETHIC that you saw and immersed your tiny feet into. I can hear Grandma now, 'YOU CAN DO IT!!'

When you build confidence in a child, there is NO telling what they can accomplish. As a Dad, I am constantly amazed and so thankful that God has you on this journey. - Daddy"

On being a perfectionist...

"Don't let the perfect get in the way of the good."

"Have you ever considered that your good is someone else's great?"

"Humility is an important characteristic in being a good friend. Everyone's answers are different and that adds to the mosaic of life. Inspire others to seek answers that will work for them because their path is for them to follow. Your way may not work for them. Be OK with that."

49

A reminder that wisdom comes from infinite sources...

"It's imperative that we capture a pearl a day
to add to our own personal treasure trove."

"Integrity is a gift from God that is His voice that
speaks to us individually. It clearly allows us
to understand our own gifts and shortcomings.
We are here to add to life, not to drain resources,
but to build a better way forward for those
that follow.

Each nugget that we pick up adds to the fab-
ric AND FOUNDATION TO MAKE OUR WORLD
SPECIFICALLY, A BETTER PLACE."

On days when indecision is a decision...

"Time has a way of eliminating options."

**"Many of life's decisions are 51/49. Grandpa
said, 'Once you have made that decision, never
look back, but instead move full steam ahead.'
A good decision with maximum effort will succeed. If you're not committed or not sure, WAIT
or make another choice."**

61

"Today is a day full of possibilities, grab one and enjoy the ride!!"

"Muhammed Ali commented, 'He who is not courageous enough to take a risk, gains nothing.' If it is your dream, believe that God placed it on your heart FOR YOU!!! Go forward with full faith and resolution!!!!"

Good - Better - Best

"Every day you wake up in the morning, everything is good. My job for the day is to make it better. At the end of the day before I close my eyes, I can tell the Lord, I did my best."

CHAPTER TWO

Family

A Moment of Reflection – A letter From Daddy to Daughter

A Warrior with a velvet touch. Princess, I do not know how to honor Him in words. As I write this, I find myself welling up in tears because I hope I have not failed Him with all that He has given me. I learned to stand on my own from Grandpa's stories of being abandoned in the barracks. I can't image the mental aspect of what he endured and overcame. Being captured and paraded in front of a town that had never seen a Black pilot, and Germans saying that they didn't know that Africa had joined WWII.

Your Grandfather made such an impression in that POW camp that 50 years later, one of the men that was in his camp, a white soldier, came to our house to tell us what Grandpa had meant to him personally and to others in his camp.

They knew what Pop had to go through and endure, but he never talked about it.

This is where I learned not to talk about my personal successes in arenas that people might misinterpret as bragging or assume didn't happen. Life is about the impossible becoming possible.

Critics will always abound, so why give them more fodder? JUST DO YOU!!!!!!!

A Moment of Reflection – A Letter From Daddy to Daughter – Part Two

Grandpa had one phrase that he would always lead with, **"IN MY OPINION."** I found this statement to be profound, dignified, singular in nature, and author-itative. This was Grandpa. Never overbearing but the weight of his words always carried the gravitas that was representative of his stature and self-confidence.

Grandma used the same phraseology when speaking from a leadership position. It was always interesting to watch her peers get quiet and listen intently to the words she was speaking.

Remember their style, which is now yours. Never raise your voice, command attention before you speak, wait until you have command of the audience, then open their eyes to possibilities. Seek to motivate and point them in an achievable direction, then inspire them to take the risk and meet the challenge.

"The strongest muscles in your body are those closest to your heart - and that is your family."

"Princess,

We learn that the things that last and have tensile strength are the virtues and values we have learned from our Nuclear Family. We wish the best for everyone but must truly respect what we have been taught and learned through discipline, structure, determination, and an understanding of each other's talent."

On family squabbles... which family doesn't have them?

"We learn how to understand differences so we can build bridges that unite."

A random text during the holidays...

Dad's often get reflective during Christmas, acknowledging that unseen forces had a hand in maneuvering us through our lives.

Love is the GREATEST GIFT GOD GAVE US. As I look around, we must be doing something right because we are surrounded by it and inhale it with every breath. It guides our choices. My Christmas "Daddyism." There is no other explanation but... We are BLESSED!!

LOVE, DADDY"

"Humans made watches. God made time— and time is not to be wasted. Dedicate your time to those who matter most."

Learn from the events of the past but incorporate what works in the present, pray, and chart a course for the future.

If you attribute all good things that happen to you as miracles, it will change your entire perspective on life.
To quote a famous group, Earth, Wind and Fire, 'Keep Your Head to The Sky.'"

Family is...

"God given. Challenging. Miraculous."

On the importance of being private....

"Grandma and Grandpa were "Mom and Pop" to an entire community, but their private lives were shared with only family and close friends that shared their same values.

Lesson: Technology is the enemy of privacy. Be mindful how you use it and who you let into your world."

"Christmas is a habitual experience.
The presents are there if you choose
to unwrap them every day."

"Every day can be Christmas, and this
mindset parallels the Friday mindset.

ADOPT AND INCORPORATE!!!!!!

It will minimize your bad days and
maximize your good days."

CHAPTER THREE

Everything Requires Balance. Work Included.

"Nature sets the example of Balance. Winter, Spring, Summer, and Fall all exist to support the next season. Part of man's responsibility is to preserve the environment for the next generation. Littering and not recognizing our responsibility to ensure the viability of the earth will fall to your generation. This will be one of your challenges over the next 20-30 years.

In ballet, the first thing you had to learn was BALANCE and the five positions. The ballet positions for arms and feet were simply known as first, second, third, fourth, and fifth. It required commitment and practice, but guess what, school work was first.

Human beings must develop intellect and physical conditioning to achieve the great things they may attempt. The confidence gained at each level girds you for the task ahead in life where it will take the full measure of your mental, physical, spiritual, and emotional self.

Work ethics come from your environment. Absorbing that people are proactive and develop their lives based on the effort that they put into any project or job. Notice there's a place and time for work and life.

"It is the parents' responsibility to help you use the guardrails of discipline, respect, and education that will allow you to meet your goals."

An excerpt from "Believe To Achieve"
by Howard "H" White

New boss, new role, new team?

"One must always be flexible to adjust to new situations.

Change is a reality of work life. There will be ups and downs. The good thing is the constant in the variable equation is YOU.

Incorporate this life lesson into your DNA, it will serve you well. 'The key is not how a person comes to you, but how you have them thinking when they leave you. Did you inspire them? Did you give them something to ponder or ideas that will expand horizons? If you did, you did your job!!!!'"

On establishing work boundaries so you can still enjoy life...

"You define what parameters you operate under."

"You have the internal fortitude and wit to 'Always Stand for Something and Not Fall for the Okie Doke.' Know the difference between short term and long term. There are NO SHORTCUTS FOR SUCCESS SO TRAIN YOURSELF FOR THE LONG TERM.

America has a capitalist system, which simply means that we pay for our goods and services. Always maintain yourself well within your financial means. Credit cards are sometimes a necessary component, but use them wisely.

Our forefathers had a layaway plan, which many stores did away with in exchange for credit. It was more beneficial to pay $25 on the hundred, which translates to $250 per $1000, which goes into their pockets.

Be a student of your finances and control your lifestyle from the prying eyes of social media."

"You can NEVER be beat if you are always willing to absorb (learn) and make something better."

"It takes a lot of courage to know that you operate out of the blessings and love quadrant of life. Some will call you naive, some will call you worse. To live in this quadrant, you have to be willing to absorb some hits and disappointments, but it will toughen you. Just like the eagle gets stronger if he doesn't catch the fish, he just dives and goes after the next one.

Eventually you will learn that not everything is intentional and people's direction is their walk in life. You will get stronger as you immerse yourself in this love quadrant."

"Some people are limited to self-defining objectives and in the end, it makes them linear. A linear opponent once defined is of absolutely no consequence on word or deed. (This is a parable, you'll learn about this soon enough).

People of linear mindsets usually call themselves practical in scope and in nature. They really are more pessimistic because they resist faith and hope as being real components in life. Without faith and hope, we would only be left to what man can do.

If we recognize that our very existence is a miracle and that we live in a country of abundance where some make a 1,000-mile trek to come here, they will realize how very fortunate they are. Is that luck, fate, or a miracle?

The answer is a miracle and that is why it is so easy to have faith because it could have been so VERY different. A linear opponent has no humility and firmly believes that they made their own way.

You will work with them and they are easy to identify. Leave them in God's hands."

Advice before a
presentation in 2013...

**"You're nervous because it
matters. If it didn't matter,
you wouldn't spend the
energy being nervous."**

On setting your own boundaries at work...

"Your LIFE IS Yours!!!!!
Judge accordingly and factor proportionally
how much of your resources it will require.

Work life balance has been disrupted by our new technology-based world where we work without walls and can do so at any time of the day or night. The union rules that previous definitions of a workday are now archaic and no longer applicable because we are no longer a manufacturing country.

It is imperative that everyone protects the sanctity of their home and private life. If they don't, the business world will take it from you - not intentionally, but it will creep in and devour your quality time with the people that you love most.

The family dinner table that was part of the nuclear secret sauce that held families together every day, has all but dissipated. Hold your family together and ensure that the much-needed casual time is integrated into everyday life. Someone in the family needs it."

A text I've received more times than I can count...
and when I don't get it, I work through lunch.

**"LUNCH TIME!!!!!!
MENTAL BREAK!!!!
Love, Daddy"**

**"If you don't give yourself a break how can you
give your family the best of you later? Find a way
to maintain you at a high level on both the job and
at home WITHOUT having to overdo either.**

Balance."

START WITH A MENTAL LUNCH BREAK. YOU DEFINE THE TIME!

WALK AWAY FROM THE DESK!!!!

Things to do when taking a mental break:

1. Say a prayer of thanks for all the miracles that have touched your life and those that are yet to come. Pray that He keeps your eyes open to see them.
2. Write a small "To Do List" centered around home

When you feel mistreated or unappreciated at work...

"If they could be you, most of them would trade places in a heartbeat. Be competitively arrogant and graciously humble!!"

"Not every encounter calls for a response. Most people just want an outlet for the frustrations that we all experience. Keep your firewall up but remember, 'The important thing is not how a person comes to you, but how they are when they leave you.'"

On office
dynamics (gossip)...

**"Never seek the
particulars because all
they can and will give
you is their perspective.
Remember that every
coin has two sides
and all you would get
is just the one side
which is IMBALANCED.**

**Inspire and
remind them they
have overcome
other hurdles!!!"**

When you realize your coworker is
playing both sides of the fence...

**"Never lose your SMILE, BUT in your mind
REMEMBER... THEY JUST SHOWED WHO
THEY ARE. USE TO YOUR ADVANTAGE!"**

**"Remember the blessings and burdens quad-
rants? This is where it really applies. Once aware,
it is easy to stay in that quadrant and now they
can't dislodge you."**

A text to get you through a rough day...

"Always remember -
There will always be times that you may lose
regardless of the endeavor, BUT you can
NEVER BE BEAT IF YOU HAVE LEARNED FROM
THE SITUATION AND APPLIED YOURSELF. If
you have done both, YOU JUST GOT BETTER!!!

SCOREBOARD:
Princess - 1 Scenario - 0
-Love, Daddy"

On navigating office politics and business in general...

"Assume the best in all things, but when it comes to business, assume that they will always protect themselves."

– Grandpa Wise, Dr. Henry A. Wise, Jr.

A reminder....

**Daddyism: Be competitively arrogant
and graciously humble.**

On workplace politics - a reminder that
non-minorities can get away with things
that minorities could never...

**"Golden child syndrome. If you build credibility,
you will have immunity - unless you're Black,
then you'll get a temporary pass at best."**

On being in control...

**"Stage your day and control your schedule,
but not based on everyone's haste!"**

Patience is the art of putting urgency in its proper perspective.

Parable translated: It will get done when I get to it!

Nature requires balance. Human achievement is always imbalanced. 80/20 rule.

(20% of the people do 80% of the work.)

CHAPTER FOUR

When Life Gives You a Right Hook

"Shake your head, dust yourself off, and once you regain your footing, take a deep breath and test the theory that, 'what didn't kill me, will make me stronger.' Thank God for helping you stop the descent and giving you a floor to stand on.

Go to a quiet place to regroup. Allow yourself recovery time and be introspective concerning the truth and honesty of your own participation that led to this moment. Know where you are and for the moment just Stand Still and listen to that little voice inside. Know which side is dominant. The blessing's side or the burden's side. One is healing and the other is self-pity.

Music, a favorite snack, and a good movie, sometimes a cry, but I promise all will be better in the morning. Just DON'T get buried in a bad place. Some people take up residence."

On letting it go and moving on...

**"Stop beating yourself up –
everyone else has moved
on to the next phase!**

**DON'T BURY YOURSELF IN
YOUR CURRENT SITUATION.
If you do, you will miss
your next opportunity."**

My grandmother's favorite poem, and one
to memorize for those tough days...

Don't Quit

When things go wrong as they sometimes will,
When the road you're trudging seems all uphill,
When the funds are low and the debts are high
And you want to smile, but you have to sigh,
When care is pressing you down a bit,
Rest if you must, but don't you quit.
Life is strange with its twists and turns
As every one of us sometimes learns
And many a failure comes about
When he might have won had he stuck it out;
Don't give up though the pace seems slow—
You may succeed with another blow.
Success is failure turned inside out—
The silver tint of the clouds of doubt,
And you never can tell just how close you are,
It may be near when it seems so far;
So stick to the fight when you're hardest hit—
It's when things seem worst that you must
not quit.

John Greenleaf Whitter

When you can't solve the problem,
adjust your perspective...

"Make the good double and cut the bad in half."

"Some People say, 'I had a Bad Day.' My reply is always, 'why not have a bad couple of hours and then ENJOY THE REST OF THE DAY!!!!!?' Turn lemons into LEMONADE."

When it is time to move on...

"Sometimes when people lie to you and are incapable of acknowledging their wrong doings, you have to forgive yourself for caring and forget them."

Eagles never carry extra weight; it would limit their soaring capability – DISCARD.

"Today is a day that your skill set will be tested. The Lord has already blessed you with the answers. In effect, it is a 'No Sweat Day.' Turn on your music and cruise.

- Love, Daddy"

Keep music, laughter, and good friends, and always say,

"Thank God I am alive."

On days when you need a little reminder...

"What are you worried about? You're blessed! You've got this."

Time has a way of putting things in historical perspective. Do you wonder why grandparents have so much wisdom???

Here is the Key:

If you do the right things as a matter of record EVERYDAY in the present, then the future will be secured and the little bumps in the road will be just bumps and easily handled.

WISDOM comes from life's experiences. Absorb, incorporate, and execute what you have learned, and you will be just fine.

God Blessed Us!

"EAGLES have adversity but in the end, it is our belief in our strength, knowledge of who we are, and knowing that no matter what, we will be WHO AND WHAT WE ARE, allows us to persevere."

Denzil Washington once said,

> "You'll never be criticized by someone doing more than you.
> You'll always be criticized by someone doing less."
> REMEMBER THAT.

Success comes from a habit of giving your best.

Choose wisely on which endeavors you select.

Partial effort guarantees partial success.

Never let someone else determine what your success looks like.

They are not you nor do they walk in your shoes.

Everyone has an opinion but only you know the true measure of yourself.

Competitively arrogant and graciously humble.

Know your gifts that God has given you and make the world a better place.

"I have never said it would be easy, but we have a gift that God gave us. We have learned from the best and they faced their adversity, survived, and then THRIVED!! So we can and will too!"

Faith!!! It is truly more than a word and if practiced makes you a more understanding and better person. This takes time but you WILL get there. Its name is WISDOM.

"Difficult times are guaranteed, but never forget to stop and count your blessings."

Aspiration and Inspiration are 100% better than the alternative. Surround yourself with people with this mindset. Modification is human. Course correction is God's Work!!!

KNOW THE DIFFERENCE

"Forgive the Past, FOCUS in the Present, and PRAY for the FUTURE!"

"Forgive the Past.

Know yourself first. Some things were trial and error, know it clearly for what it was. Incorporate the nutrition garnered from the past and then discard the waste.

Focus in the Present.

Clearly understand that TIME is never the problem and that solutions reside in your Patience and Perseverance. Use our YODA!!!!! Then Become your OWN SME (Subject Matter Expert).

Pray for The Future

God First. Family second. Love, music, and great times are in store for you!!! This I know!!"

"Count Your blessings in the best of times and it will fortify you to handle the turbulence that life throws at you. LOVE EVERYDAY!!"

When the year was off to a tough start...

"Find a laugh in difficult times and KNOW THAT THAT IS HOW GRANDMA DID IT. She would say 'this is nothing,' and handle it and move forward with resolute determination. SHE LET NOTHING ROCK HER BOAT! Daddy flicks troubles off my shoulders because I know that I am the BIGGER BEAR, regardless of the situation. And the choice is mine, guided by the hand of The Almighty!!

Put a smile on that face and say, 'LOOK OUT world, HERE WE COME!!'

Love, Daddy"

When life gives you a right hook...

Absorb it and that will prove your strength. Study where it came from and that will provide wisdom. Never retaliate, just overcome. People get sucked into revenge, just overcome.

You took the hit and are still here

You ARE THE BIGGER BEAR!!!!!

Don't beat yourself up today for what you didn't do yesterday. Focus on today and what you can do better tomorrow.

CHAPTER FIVE

Marriage, Relationships, Heartbreak, and Loss

On marriage....

"There are challenges that you two will face in your life. The two of you are easy targets - Protect your home. The adjustments necessary to protect each other become the LAWS OF THE RELATIONSHIP."

ABSOLUTELY

On Human Distractions...

"Even if you don't water it, failure to shut it down can lead to discord. A cactus doesn't need water to grow, but it can inflict significant pain."

Grandma's Philosophy

Don't Mess with my Husband/Wife.

Don't Mess with my Children.

Don't Mess with My Money.

"People will do and say anything, but if they are outside the borders of respect, it has to be dealt with."

**"You two are MARRIED!!!
Work this out head on AND
GET THROUGH THIS!!!!"**

Lesson: Marriage means not giving
up even when things get hard.

On where to find peace and how
to measure success...

**"Be content in the present. Jobs can be
transitory and expiration dates are in someone
else's hands, but HOME is FOREVER."**

Setting the tone for your day is in your mindset...

"Today is the best day of your life. Put all your 'best practice skill sets' into play and give the people you interact with the gift of possibility by turning it into reality!!!!

My Daddyism for the day!!"

It's always a JOY when you see the light in someone from something you said or did. Becoming the rocket fuel to inspire someone to believe in their particular course is why we are here and how we can judge our day!

This is what was meant by the phrase, "It is better to give than to receive."

**Forgive the past.
Live in the present.
Plan for the future.**

On days when you need to remember your value...

"They are a compliment, not a supplement...you are not deficient."

If you cut your chains

You will be free

If you cut your roots

You DIE.

-Unknown

You can always choose to be free.

A Daughter-ism...because the wisdom rubs off overtime!

"Your relationships are only as deep as what you're willing to expose within yourself."

– DWP

A friend-ism on who is most important in a relationship...

"Divert your gaze, the only person who needs to be pleased is me."

- Dr. Rabiatu Barrie

Lesson: Focus on who is important – the others don't count.

"At the apex of a triangle is where God sits in the relationship. Each party is at the bottom looking up. If you both simultaneously climb toward the top and keep that your objective, it will bring you closer to God and to each other!

God is the epitome of LOVE.

Always be the Subject Matter Expert (SME).

-Daddy"

On solving a quarrel...

"If you separate the topic
from the emotion, then you
can solve the issue."

"It is essential that you
remove the issue
from between the
two of you and
place it on your wall,
and both of you look
at it from the same side.

You'll be wonderfully
surprised that the viewpoint
now will be close."

A word applicable to many things...

"Just because you can doesn't mean you should."

On staying focused on who matters most...

"Don't try to make everyone happy because everyone doesn't count."

We have a limited amount of emotional capacity and intellectual properties each day. Treat it like the TREASURE it is and Focus on what you can affect.

From Daddy to Daughter, on days
when time is the best healer...

"It is your **BEDROOM!!!! DO NOT LEAVE IT, and
a respectable man will never let you. That
is what sofas are for until the fog lifts."**

"Power couples
never fall for
the okey-doke."

"Be vulnerable, not stupid."

Empathy and humility are strengths. Although people often mistake these characteristics as weakness, they are some of the most valuable traits that the Lord gave us.

On being a good partner..

"When challenges arise, using your skill set of love and belief, shower your house in those characteristics and never keep a rain cloud over you or him. As you rise, you will lift him. It is a formula that is unbeatable. Love has longevity. Pain, doubt, and other negatives are all short term in duration. Eagles soar above the storm."

143

"Your irresponsibility will always become someone else's responsibility. Be responsible. Be accountable."

- Buckhead Church 9.11.12

Think before you speak...

**"Words never said,
never have to be apologized for."**

"You can't be the arson and the fireman too."

"Don't give up on the good just because it's dark at night. It is always dark before it's light."

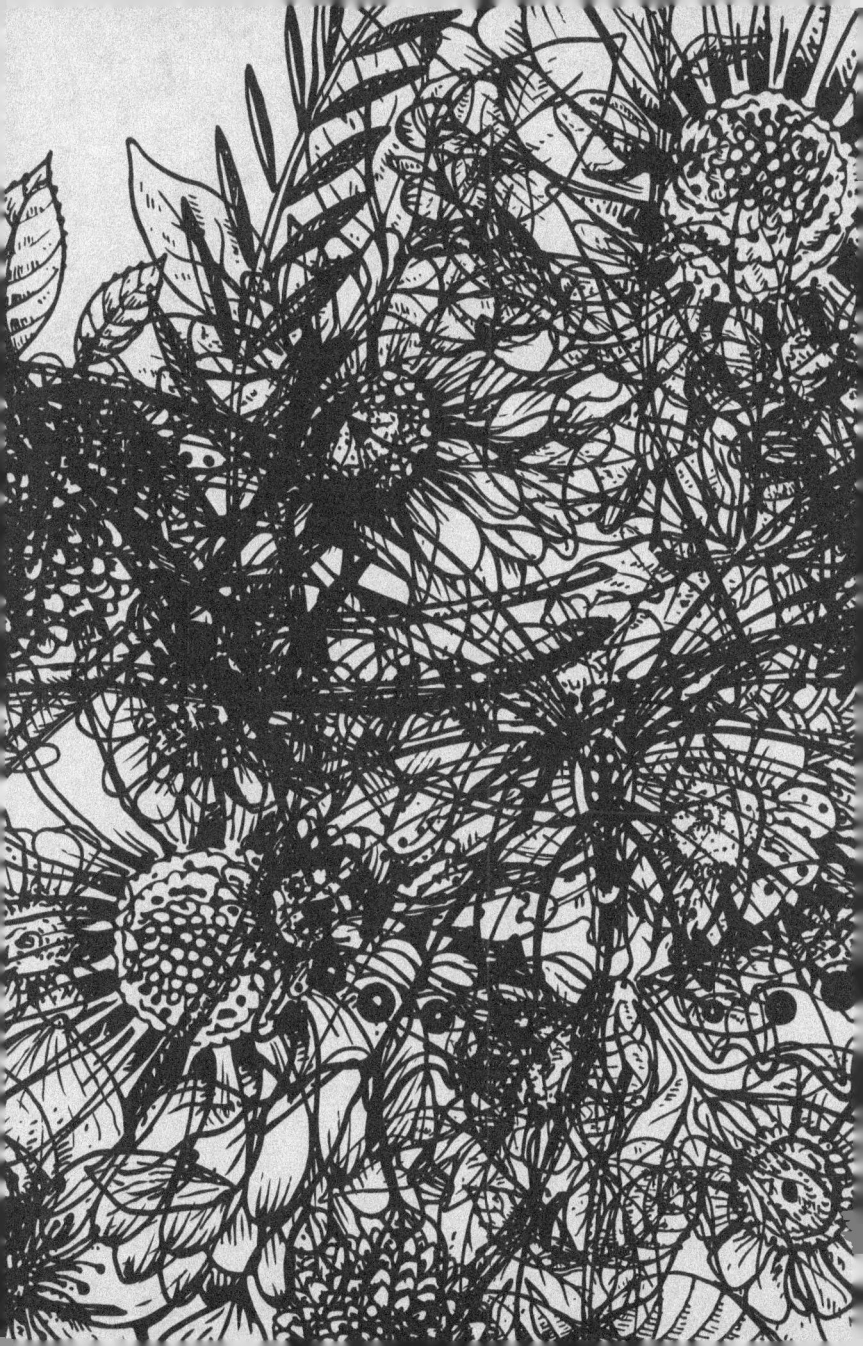

"Don't pitch what you can't catch."

Follow the old adage of "Do unto others as you would have them do unto you."

CHAPTER SIX

Kool-Aid

Daddyism:

**"When faced with a challenge,
be the Bigger Bear!!"**

**Remember: Fairness only comes when it is
your hand on the knife that cuts the cake.
Otherwise just be happy to get a slice.**

**When in question, just think,
"What would Grandma do?"**

**The answer will lead to a reliable course
of action that will NEVER FAIL!!**

"Pressure makes diamonds, and we are always at our best in these situations.

—Love, Daddy"

"It is important to know WHO you are and the characteristics that run through you. Outstanding character and qualities run through your bloodline. Reflect upon these and know the mantle upon which we stand."

"Hi Princess,
Your energy level to meet the demands of the day
are based on your reservoir. There should be no ups
and no downs because that will drain that reservoir.
You must rebuild your tolerance level, whereas
before you may have taken it for granted by being a
problem solver. Now don't overextend and that will
become your new norm. Others will have to figure it
out and you just manicure the results or send them
back to the drawing board. DON'T TAKE ON THEIR
WORK! This will make your life much easier.
-Love, Daddy"

Masterpiece on Balance

Special Daddy Note:
When facing a tough environment...

**"First: Wrap yourself in prayer and His protection from the crown of your head to the soles of your feet. That is impenetrable.
Second: Eagles soar to places others can't envision. Reside there with your high level of professionalism.
Third: Keep your smile and demeanor. Everything will settle down in a way that will be beneficial for you.
Fourth: Take lunch Every Day! Keep music in your head and love in your heart. Anchor on something that makes you smile and go there for 45 min. Daddy's remedy!!
-Love you!"**

"Hi Princess,
You sounded like you were still in a decision-making mindset. Remember, most decisions are 51/49 and do require some painstaking thought. In the end, the right decision is made because you made it – trust your judgment!!
-Love, Daddy"

160

"Hi Princess,

Daddyism: Never ever BEAT YOURSELF! Doubt is the CANCER that will erode all of your confidence, beliefs, and hopes. It ultimately will rob you of your faith in the unseen, which is the essence of GOD'S GREATEST GIFT TO MANKIND, LOVE.

It is better to fortify your faith and set your feet on that ground because you give breath and life to the miracles and possibilities that are yours to claim. I can live with being proven wrong or disappointed. As opposed to having no faith and always chasing and looking for something negative that may or may not exist. It will destroy the precious flower of love and lead you into self-protectiveness and in the end, unhappiness. Nothing good comes from that mindset.

—Love, Daddy"

"What is true
should never be
hidden, to even
try is a reflection
of their souls."

My dad just being cheesy...

The most famous party mix of all is Kool-Aid. It always brings a smile!

CHAPTER SEVEN

Keep a Song in Your Heart

Joy & Pain
By Maze

Remember when you first found love how you felt
so good
Kind that last forever more so you thought it would
Suddenly the things you see got you hurt so bad
How come the things that make us happy make
us sad
Well it seems to me that
Joy and pain are like sunshine and rain
Joy and pain are like sunshine and rain
Love can be bitter love can be sweet
Sometimes devotion and sometimes deceit
The ones that you care for give you so much pain
Oh but it's alright they're both one in the same
Don't it seem we go through life going up and down
Seems the things that turn you on turn you around
Always hurting each other if it ain't one thing
it's another
But when the world is down on you love's
somewhere around
Well it seems to me that
Joy and pain are like sunshine and rain
Joy and pain are like sunshine and rain
Joy and pain are like sunshine and rain
Joy and pain are like sunshine and rain
Over and over you can be sure
There will be sorrow but you will endure
Where there's a flower there's the sun and the rain

Oh and it's wonderful there both one in the same
Joy and pain are like sunshine and rain
Joy and pain are like sunshine and rain
Joy and pain are like sunshine and rain
Joy and pain are like sunshine and rain

Baby the Rain Must Fall
By: Glenn Yarbrough

Some men climb a mountain,
Some men swim the sea,
Some men fly above the sky:
They are what they must be.
But, baby the rain must fall,
Baby, the wind must blow,
Wherever my heart leads me
Baby, I must go, baby I must go.
I do not love for silver,
I do not love for gold,
My heart is mine to give away,
It never will be sold.
So, baby the rain must fall,
Baby, the wind must blow,
Wherever my heart leads me
Baby I must go, baby I must go.
I am not rich or famous:
But who can ever tell?
I don't know now what waits for me
Maybe heaven, maybe hell.
Baby, the rain must fall,
Baby, the wind must blow,
Wherever my heart leads me
Baby I must go, baby I must go.

The perfect ending to my Father's note:
"WHEREVER MY HEART LEADS
ME, BABY I MUST GO!!"

About the Author

DeShaun N. Wise Porter is the **Global Head of Diversity, Equity, Inclusion & Engagement** at a major hospitality company. She serves as a strategic thought leader and internal consultant who is responsible for developing  and executing holistic and integrated strategies that are aligned with Hilton's shared values, and contributing to the building of a diverse, engaged, and high-performing organization. Prior to this appointment, she served as the VP, HR Consulting partnering with C-Suite leaders to drive and implement transformational talent initiatives focused on attracting, developing, and retaining high potentials and top performers.

A passionate leader with extensive experience in driving culture change and creating opportunities that accelerate the growth of talent through differentiated talent models and scalable development programs. Her work has centered on leading global transformation initiatives, managing merger and acquisition processes, overseeing the implementation of core technologies, and developing teams across the globe. She served as an advisor on the integration of market-based compensation, implementation of an advanced HR Information Systems, as well as a key architect in designing the high-performing learning organization at Kimberly-Clark, which included the first global learning management system and language-learning program. Her global business acumen paired with her cultural dexterity positioned her for short-term assignments in Seoul, South Korea, Istanbul, Turkey, and Medellin, Colombia.

DeShaun is a graduate of Florida State University where she studied Multinational Business Operations and Finance. She holds a Professional in Human Resources (PHR) Certification from the HR Certificate Institute, a SHRM-Certified Professional (SHRM-CP) from the Society for Human Resource Management, and a Human Capital Strategist Certification from the Human Capital Institute. She is currently on the Board of Directors for FAIR Girls, Inc. and an active member of the Society for Human Resources Management, Alpha Kappa Alpha Sorority, Incorporated, and The Links, Incorporated. She is active throughout her community and serves as a youth mentor and advocate for abused and molested children.

DeShaun resides in Washington, D.C. with her husband, Dr. Fernando A. Porter, M.D., sons Princeton Antonio and Braylon Alexander, and fur baby Marley.

When she is not spending time with family and friends or participating in civic activities, she enjoys shopping, reading, and embracing other cultures through travel.

Book Summary

This book captures the dreams parents have for their children. Do you want the best for them? How will that happen?

- Do you want to protect them?
- How will you do it?
- Do you want them to be successful at their endeavors?
- How can you ensure that?
- Do you want them to be well thought of in the community?
- What are the best avenues?
- Do you want to shield them from heartbreak?
- How can you do that?
- Do you want them to understand the importance of God in their life?

- How do you emphasize that?

It was the end of 2015, just minutes before midnight the phone rang and I was told he was being rushed to the hospital – pain in chest, sweating feverishly, and struggling to breath. Still in motion, but I was panicking. Standing tall at six feet, two inches with a larger-than-life smile and words for every occasion, how could anything take him down? I was scared at what my father was going through and the thought of life without him paralyzed me. After all, he was my hero and heroes are untouchable. During one of the longest rides of my life [to the hospital] I was overtaken with emotion. I experienced a condensed reel of our conversations, our laughs, our experiences, but what stood out was his advice. As my voice left my body, my thoughts echoed loudly, "You didn't write the book. How will you preserve the wisdom?"

Wise Porter takes a walk-through time-sharing intimate daddy-daughter quotes and conversations that yield advice and provide inspiration. Collected over several years are lessons that were secretly captured during various phases of life. Both power and comfort reside in the stories we remember or the conversations we had, but the ability to recount some of the details can stray over time but this collection captures it, timelessly.

These Daddyisms were planted with the hope that they would become a foundation and a source of direction. Over the years, I've found both wisdom and comfort in the random texts, early morning calls, and general conversations. We hope this serves as a reminder to all parents – although it appears your children are preoccupied, they hear you and it is your wisdom they will call on when they need it.

As a new mom, this guidance has an even deeper meaning for me. They have been my roadmap through thick and thin, and I look forward to sharing them with my children and with all of you!

About My Father, Keith Evan Wise

Some call it an autobiography but in his words, it is "A Life Full Of Miracles"...

The first miracle was that I was born on June 4th, 1951 in Freedman's hospital (now Howard University Hospital) in Washington, DC. My parents were Roberta and Dr. Henry A. Wise, Jr. These two individuals were role models for me and many others throughout my lifetime. Mom was short of stature, full of love, elegant in her mannerisms, and a force to be reckoned with if you messed with her husband, her family, or her money. She was from Leavenworth, Kansas. Pop was from Cape Charles, Virginia and he became a Tuskegee Fighter Pilot. He was quiet and stoic but had a commanding presence and took his skills to become a Physician in Prince George's County, Maryland. Together they established the Maryland Debutantes in the early 1960s and were well-known for their service to the community. Mom and Pop also gave my brother and I a great understanding that we are a part of something bigger and that love and faith are never to be compromised. Laughter and a hug was Mom's medicine, and some bread pudding helped as well. Pop had a strength that could only come from being in a barracks alone as a Black Fighter Pilot while others refused to share the barracks with him.

A quick aside: Pop's P-51 Mustang was shot down on Aug 26, 1944 and he was captured by the Germans. They said to him, "For you the war is over." Eventually the Russians freed the prisoners and he returned to America. Over 50 plus years later a white soldier found Pop and came to the house to say, "he was one of the most remarkable of men he had ever met."

There's more to the story but this demonstrated what he always said, "Skip (my nickname), it's what people remember about your interaction that is important." Translated to, "DeShaun I have always said, 'It's not how a person comes to you but were they inspired when they leave you.'"

In 1956, my family moved to Carsondale, Maryland. When they say it takes a whole village to raise a child, it is true and I am a product of that. The summer of Mom's passing in 2019, I took my family back to my roots where they saw firsthand the warmth, love and treasure we had developed in our community. If any of you happen to read this, thank you for helping to make me who I am. I carried that spirit with me everywhere.

Grade school was Holy Redeemer in Washington, DC. At that time Nuns were the primary teachers and boy was I scared of them! Strict was an understatement. If God had them on His side, then He certainly would have no problem with me. It wasn't until third grade when I saw an "ankle" under the nun's robes that I finally realized they were women. You do learn things as you grow up!!

St. John's Military High School (1965-1969) I wore the military uniform every day and in my senior year, I won the Top Captain award for our performance in the spring. Won academic scholarships and played football and Varsity basketball and we were ranked fourth in the city. I also had offers from West Point and the Air Force Academy but chose a path less trodden.

I attended Oberlin College from 1969-1971. (Fun fact, we won the OAC Conference in 1969 and Oberlin has not won since). I transferred to The University of Maryland in 1974 graduating with a BA in Psychology. While there I served as President of the University Commuters Association in 1973 representing 80% of the student population of 35,000 students. I instituted the ORIGINAL Shuttle Bus System in response to rapes on campus. To fund this effort, we held a show that included Earth, Wind and Fire for students and the proceeds went for two vans that would drive through the multiple school parking lots at specific times and pick up and return students to their cars. The credit for bringing this group and others goes to Pat Leer, who ended up being the road manager for Hall and Oates. We had plans to extend throughout the local apartment complexes as well.

This also prompted the administration to hire the First Director of Commuter Affairs, Mr. Mark Hardwick, to represent the commuting population. At the time the University of Michigan was the only other school in the country to have this type of position. I arranged for ten charter buses to attend the last Bullets game in Baltimore before they were to move to the New Capital Centre in Landover, Maryland. It was full of refreshments from the fraternities and the Bullet's management were so impressed I was offered a job as a Group Sales Manager in the New Capital Centre. His name was Chip Reed and I thank him to this day for the experience.

Xerox was next and the training center was top shelf. I attended the Professional Selling Skills Class in 1976. I want to thank my good friend James Brown who introduced me to Barry Rand, who interviewed me and offered me the Job. JB, you see on NFL football, and Barry Rand who recently passed also became head of AARP. I sold the Washington Redskins their first color copier in Ashburn, Va. JB, once again thanks and we can still see our mothers sitting in the stands!

In 1980, I started with my first of many positions with Amtrak. There I had the pleasure of meeting so many greats, as New York Penn station was the start and end for all great tours. I shifted to New Jersey Transit in 1993 after accepting a buyout from Amtrak. Life led me back to my roots where I joined IKON Office Solutions followed by Toshiba and Canon, where I was quickly recognized as #1 in the country for Sales. While I am proud of all my career achievements, they pale in comparison to my best work.

I have many personal miracles and highlights in my life, that I can count all joy:

- **1982 —** March 8th at 7:24 pm, God brought my angel to earth. I saw the nurse crossing the floor with a little bundle and before she could put her down, I had her in my arms. There were no words for that moment, all I could say was, "Thank you God" as I counted all fingers and toes.

- **1999 —** The year I met my wife. We never actually dated, God just said this was my answer to my missing rib. Deb was there EVERY weekend to take care of Pop and when he passed in May 2003, we continued with Mom until 2019, when at 103 she went to join him. I never had to ask, and I am eternally grateful that she allowed me so much time to focus on taking care of both of them. Deb, I can't thank you enough!!

- **2000 —** Princess' High School graduation, this was mind-blowing on so many levels. She is 5 star, she's beautiful, smart, dedicated, focused, and God-fearing. Despite my efforts for her to choose Howard, she set her eyes on Florida State University.

- **2003 —** Pop has more than done his job and I promised him, I would take care of Mom and keep the family together!! I miss him. He was a GIANT among men.

- **2004 —** Princess' college graduation, HOORAY!!!!!!!!!

- **2005 —** May 14th, I married my Bride! God ordained this but I thank Him every day for her! She is a 12 on a 10 scale, she loves Princess and now we are grandparents, retired and blessed!!!!! She is my Miracle!!

- **2015 —** The year prostate cancer became a reality. I never wavered in my belief that I could overcome it, but with my schedule there were some hard decisions to be made. God would have to guide me through just like He has done so many other times.

- **2015 —** The year I gained a son. Fernando was a natural fit and Grandma loved him as did Deb and I. He asked for DeShaun's hand in marriage, and I knew God had interceded again and that all would be fine. I kept my health quiet until the last couple of weeks as to not allow it to be a thief of our joy.

Fernando was the right one and we both laughed because every year of her life I have bought Princess a bear of some kind. Fernando said to me, "Pop you don't have to do that anymore because she has her own personal Grizzly Bear." I love my son because he too is a Miracle.

- **2016 –** Feb. 16th. WEDDING DAY!!!!! MIRACLE!!!! Jamaica!!! I MADE IT!!!!!!!!

- **2019 –** Feb RETIRED!!!!!!!!! MIRACLE!!!!!!!!!!!!!!!!!

- **2021 –** May 3rd MIRACLE! GRANDSON: PRINCETON ANTONIO PORTER!!!!!!!!!!!!!

  THE MIRACLES CONTINUE...stay tuned!